The Stork's Assistant

A Surrogacy Journey Journal

Sometimes when making something so **precious**, **beautiful**, and **unique**, it takes an extra helping **heart**.

Meet your Surrogate

Paste 3x5 photo of Surrogate here!

And Her Family

Paste 3x5 photo of Surrogate's Family here!

Surrogate Information

Name: _____

Age: _____

Family Members: _____

Pets: _____

Located in: _____

Favorite Food: _____

Reason she wanted to be a surrogate:

_____

_____

_____

Why is this the perfect match?

_____

_____

_____

_____

Thoughts on the journey so far:

_____

_____

_____

_____

_____

_____

_____

_____

Timeline Milestones

We matched on: _____

Contracts were signed on: _____

Medical Clearance on: _____

Legal Clearance on: _____

Saline Sono Hysterogram on: _____

Timeline Milestones

Psych Evaluation on: _____

Baseline Ultrasound on: _____

Started Medication on: _____

Lining Check on: _____

Final Lining Check on: _____

Milestone Pictures

The medications have arrived!

Paste 3x3 photo of meds here!

The 1st Shot!

Paste 3x3 photo of 1st shot here!

Milestone Pictures

Baseline Ultrasound

Place 3x3 photo of baseline US here!

Baseline was _____

Lining Check

Place 3x3 photo of lining check here!

Lining was _____

I Can't Keep Calm.
It's Transfer Day!

Place 3x3 photo of embryo here!

Embryologist Name: _____

Reproductive Endocrinologist: _____

Embryo Stage: _____

Embryo Quality: _____

Thoughts:

_____

_____

_____

Pictures of Transfer Day!

WE'RE PREGNANT!

Home Pregnancy Test

Place 3x3 photo of home pregnancy test here!

Date: _____

_____Days Past Transfer

WE'RE PREGNANT!

Date of First Beta: _____

_____ days past transfer

Beta is _____

Date of Second Beta: _____

_____ days past transfer

Beta is _____

Date of Third Beta: _____

_____ days past transfer

Beta is _____

Month 1

Week 1 - Week 4

Journal Page

Week 1

Appointments:

Monday	Tuesday	Wednesday	Thursday	Friday	Saturday	Sunday

Notes:

_____

_____

_____

_____

Week 1

Med Calendar:

Monday	Tuesday	Wednesday	Thursday	Friday	Saturday	Sunday

Week 2

Appointments:

Monday	Tuesday	Wednesday	Thursday	Friday	Saturday	Sunday

Notes:

_____

_____

_____

_____

Week 2

Med Calendar:

Monday	Tuesday	Wednesday	Thursday	Friday	Saturday	Sunday

Week 3

Appointments:

Monday	Tuesday	Wednesday	Thursday	Friday	Saturday	Sunday

Notes:

_____

_____

_____

_____

Week 3

Med Calendar:

Monday	Tuesday	Wednesday	Thursday	Friday	Saturday	Sunday

Week 4

Appointments:

Monday	Tuesday	Wednesday	Thursday	Friday	Saturday	Sunday

Notes:

_____

_____

_____

_____

Week 4

Med Calendar:

Monday	Tuesday	Wednesday	Thursday	Friday	Saturday	Sunday

Pictures

Baby is the size of a Poppy Seed

Thoughts and Feelings:

_____

_____

_____

_____

_____

_____

Cravings:

_____

_____

_____

_____

Month 2

Week 5 - Week 8

Journal Page

Week 5

Appointments:

Monday	Tuesday	Wednesday	Thursday	Friday	Saturday	Sunday

Notes:

_____

_____

_____

_____

Week 5

Med Calendar:

Monday	Tuesday	Wednesday	Thursday	Friday	Saturday	Sunday

Pictures

Baby is the size of an Apple Seed

Thoughts and Feelings:

_____

_____

_____

_____

_____

_____

Cravings:

_____

_____

_____

_____

Week 6

Appointments:

Monday	Tuesday	Wednesday	Thursday	Friday	Saturday	Sunday

Notes:

_____

_____

_____

_____

Week 6

Med Calendar:

Monday	Tuesday	Wednesday	Thursday	Friday	Saturday	Sunday

Pictures

Baby is the size of a Sweet Pea

Thoughts and Feelings:

_____

_____

_____

_____

_____

Cravings:

_____

_____

_____

_____

Week 7

Appointments:

Monday	Tuesday	Wednesday	Thursday	Friday	Saturday	Sunday

Notes:

_____

_____

_____

_____

Week 7

Med Calendar:

Monday	Tuesday	Wednesday	Thursday	Friday	Saturday	Sunday

Pictures

Baby is the size of a Blueberry

Thoughts and Feelings:

_____

_____

_____

_____

_____

_____

Cravings:

_____

_____

_____

_____

Week 8

Appointments:

Monday	Tuesday	Wednesday	Thursday	Friday	Saturday	Sunday

Notes:

_____

_____

_____

_____

Week 8

Med Calendar:

Monday	Tuesday	Wednesday	Thursday	Friday	Saturday	Sunday

Pictures

Baby is the size of a Raspberry

Thoughts and Feelings:

_____

_____

_____

_____

_____

_____

Cravings:

_____

_____

_____

_____

Month 3

Week 9 - Week 12

Journal Page

Week 9

Appointments:

Monday	Tuesday	Wednesday	Thursday	Friday	Saturday	Sunday

Notes:

_____

_____

_____

_____

Week 9

Med Calendar:

Monday	Tuesday	Wednesday	Thursday	Friday	Saturday	Sunday

Pictures

Baby is the size of a Green Olive

Thoughts and Feelings:

_____

_____

_____

_____

_____

_____

Cravings:

_____

_____

_____

_____

Week 10

Appointments:

Monday	Tuesday	Wednesday	Thursday	Friday	Saturday	Sunday

Notes:

_____

_____

_____

_____

Week 10

Med Calendar:

Monday	Tuesday	Wednesday	Thursday	Friday	Saturday	Sunday

Pictures

Baby is the size of a Prune

Thoughts and Feelings:

_____

_____

_____

_____

_____

Cravings:

_____

_____

_____

_____

Week 11

Appointments:

Monday	Tuesday	Wednesday	Thursday	Friday	Saturday	Sunday

Notes:

_____

_____

_____

_____

Week 11

Med Calendar:

Monday	Tuesday	Wednesday	Thursday	Friday	Saturday	Sunday

Pictures

Baby is the size of a Lime

Thoughts and Feelings:

_____

_____

_____

_____

_____

_____

Cravings:

_____

_____

_____

_____

Week 12

Appointments:

Monday	Tuesday	Wednesday	Thursday	Friday	Saturday	Sunday

Notes:

_____

_____

_____

_____

Week 12

Med Calendar:

Monday	Tuesday	Wednesday	Thursday	Friday	Saturday	Sunday

Pictures

Baby is the size of a Plum

Thoughts and Feelings:

_____

_____

_____

_____

_____

_____

Cravings:

_____

_____

_____

_____

Month 4

Week 13 - Week 16

Journal Page

Week 13

Appointments:

Monday	Tuesday	Wednesday	Thursday	Friday	Saturday	Sunday

Notes:

_____

_____

_____

_____

Baby is the size of a Peach

Thoughts and Feelings:

_____

_____

_____

_____

_____

_____

Cravings:

_____

_____

_____

_____

Pictures

Journal Page

Week 14

Appointments:

Monday	Tuesday	Wednesday	Thursday	Friday	Saturday	Sunday

Notes:

_____

_____

_____

_____

Baby is the size of a Lemon

Thoughts and Feelings:

_____

_____

_____

_____

_____

_____

Cravings:

_____

_____

_____

_____

Pictures

Journal Page

Week 15

Appointments:

Monday	Tuesday	Wednesday	Thursday	Friday	Saturday	Sunday

Notes:

_____

_____

_____

_____

Baby is the size of an orange

Thoughts and Feelings:

_____

_____

_____

_____

_____

_____

Cravings:

_____

_____

_____

_____

Pictures

Journal Page

Week 16

Appointments:

Monday	Tuesday	Wednesday	Thursday	Friday	Saturday	Sunday

Notes:

_____

_____

_____

_____

Baby is the size of an Avocado

Thoughts and Feelings:

_____

_____

_____

_____

_____

_____

Cravings:

_____

_____

_____

_____

Pictures

Journal Page

Month 5

Week 17 - Week 20

Journal Page

Week 17

Appointments:

Monday	Tuesday	Wednesday	Thursday	Friday	Saturday	Sunday

Notes:

_____

_____

_____

_____

Baby is the size of an onion

Thoughts and Feelings:

_____

_____

_____

_____

_____

_____

Cravings:

_____

_____

_____

_____

Pictures

Journal Page

Week 18

Appointments:

Monday	Tuesday	Wednesday	Thursday	Friday	Saturday	Sunday

Notes:

_____

_____

_____

_____

Baby is the size of a sweet potato

Thoughts and Feelings:

_____

_____

_____

_____

_____

_____

Cravings:

_____

_____

_____

_____

Pictures

Journal Page

Week 19

Appointments:

Monday	Tuesday	Wednesday	Thursday	Friday	Saturday	Sunday

Notes:

_____

_____

_____

_____

Baby is the size of a Mango

Thoughts and Feelings:

_____

_____

_____

_____

_____

_____

Cravings:

_____

_____

_____

_____

Pictures

Journal Page

Week 20

Appointments:

Monday	Tuesday	Wednesday	Thursday	Friday	Saturday	Sunday

Notes:

_____

_____

_____

_____

Baby is the size of a Banana

Thoughts and Feelings:

_____

_____

_____

_____

_____

_____

Cravings:

_____

_____

_____

_____

Pictures

Journal Page

Month 6

Week 21 - Week 24

Journal Page

Week 21

Appointments:

Monday	Tuesday	Wednesday	Thursday	Friday	Saturday	Sunday

Notes:

_____

_____

_____

_____

Baby is the size of a Pomegranate

Thoughts and Feelings:

_____

_____

_____

_____

_____

_____

Cravings:

_____

_____

_____

_____

Pictures

Journal Page

Week 22

Appointments:

Monday	Tuesday	Wednesday	Thursday	Friday	Saturday	Sunday

Notes:

_____

_____

_____

Baby is the size of a Papaya

Thoughts and Feelings:

_____

_____

_____

_____

_____

_____

Cravings:

_____

_____

_____

_____

Pictures

Journal Page

_____

_____

_____

_____

_____

_____

_____

_____

_____

_____

_____

_____

_____

_____

Week 23

Appointments:

Monday	Tuesday	Wednesday	Thursday	Friday	Saturday	Sunday

Notes:

_____

_____

_____

Baby is the size of a Grapefruit

Thoughts and Feelings:

_____

_____

_____

_____

_____

_____

Cravings:

_____

_____

_____

_____

Pictures

Journal Page

Week 24

Appointments:

Monday	Tuesday	Wednesday	Thursday	Friday	Saturday	Sunday

Notes:

_____

_____

_____

Baby is the size of a Cantaloupe

Thoughts and Feelings:

_____

_____

_____

_____

_____

_____

Cravings:

_____

_____

_____

_____

Pictures

Journal Page

Month 7

Week 25 - Week 28

Journal Page

Week 25

Appointments:

Monday	Tuesday	Wednesday	Thursday	Friday	Saturday	Sunday

Notes:

_____

_____

_____

Baby is the size of a Cauliflower

Thoughts and Feelings:

_____

_____

_____

_____

_____

_____

Cravings:

_____

_____

_____

_____

Pictures

Journal Page

Week 26

Appointments:

Monday	Tuesday	Wednesday	Thursday	Friday	Saturday	Sunday

Notes:

_____

_____

_____

Baby is the size of a Head of Lettuce

Thoughts and Feelings:

_____

_____

_____

_____

_____

_____

Cravings:

_____

_____

_____

_____

Pictures

Journal Page

Week 27

Appointments:

Monday	Tuesday	Wednesday	Thursday	Friday	Saturday	Sunday

Notes:

_____

_____

_____

Baby is the size of a Rutabaga

Thoughts and Feelings:

_____

_____

_____

_____

_____

Cravings:

_____

_____

_____

_____

Pictures

Journal Page

Week 28

Appointments:

Monday	Tuesday	Wednesday	Thursday	Friday	Saturday	Sunday

Notes:

_____

_____

_____

Baby is the size of an Eggplant

Thoughts and Feelings:

_____

_____

_____

_____

_____

_____

Cravings:

_____

_____

_____

_____

Pictures

Journal Page

Month 8

Week 29 - Week 32

Journal Page

_____

_____

_____

_____

_____

_____

_____

_____

_____

_____

_____

_____

_____

Week 29

Appointments:

Monday	Tuesday	Wednesday	Thursday	Friday	Saturday	Sunday

Notes:

_____

_____

_____

Baby is the size of an Acorn Squash

Thoughts and Feelings:

_____

_____

_____

_____

_____

_____

Cravings:

_____

_____

_____

_____

Pictures

Journal Page

Week 30

Appointments:

Monday	Tuesday	Wednesday	Thursday	Friday	Saturday	Sunday

Notes:

_____

_____

_____

Baby is the size of a Cucumber

Thoughts and Feelings:

_____

_____

_____

_____

_____

_____

Cravings:

_____

_____

_____

_____

Pictures

Journal Page

_____

_____

_____

_____

_____

_____

_____

_____

_____

_____

_____

_____

Week 31

Appointments:

Monday	Tuesday	Wednesday	Thursday	Friday	Saturday	Sunday

Notes:

_____

_____

_____

Baby is the size of a Pineapple

Thoughts and Feelings:

_____

_____

_____

_____

_____

_____

Cravings:

_____

_____

_____

_____

Pictures

Journal Page

_____

_____

_____

_____

_____

_____

_____

_____

_____

_____

_____

_____

_____

_____

Week 32

Appointments:

Monday	Tuesday	Wednesday	Thursday	Friday	Saturday	Sunday

Notes:

_____

_____

_____

Baby is the size of a Yellow Squash

Thoughts and Feelings:

_____

_____

_____

_____

_____

_____

Cravings:

_____

_____

_____

_____

Pictures

Journal Page

Month 9

Week 33 - Week 36

Journal Page

Week 33

Appointments:

Monday	Tuesday	Wednesday	Thursday	Friday	Saturday	Sunday

Notes:

_____

_____

_____

Baby is the size of a Durian

Thoughts and Feelings:

_____

_____

_____

_____

_____

_____

Cravings:

_____

_____

_____

_____

Pictures

Journal Page

Week 34

Appointments:

Monday	Tuesday	Wednesday	Thursday	Friday	Saturday	Sunday

Notes:

_____

_____

_____

Baby is the size of a Butternut Squash

Thoughts and Feelings:

_____

_____

_____

_____

_____

_____

Cravings:

_____

_____

_____

_____

Pictures

Journal Page

_____

_____

_____

_____

_____

_____

_____

_____

_____

_____

_____

_____

Week 35

Appointments:

Monday	Tuesday	Wednesday	Thursday	Friday	Saturday	Sunday

Notes:

_____

_____

_____

Baby is the size of a Coconut

Thoughts and Feelings:

_____

_____

_____

_____

_____

_____

Cravings:

_____

_____

_____

_____

Pictures

Journal Page

Week 36

Appointments:

Monday	Tuesday	Wednesday	Thursday	Friday	Saturday	Sunday

Notes:

_____

_____

_____

Baby is the size of a Honeydew Melon

Thoughts and Feelings:

_____

_____

_____

_____

_____

_____

Cravings:

_____

_____

_____

_____

Pictures

Journal Page

_____

_____

_____

_____

_____

_____

_____

_____

_____

_____

_____

_____

_____

_____

Month 10

Week 37 - Week 40

Journal Page

Week 37

Appointments:

Monday	Tuesday	Wednesday	Thursday	Friday	Saturday	Sunday

Notes:

_____

_____

_____

Baby is the size of a Winter Melon

Thoughts and Feelings:

_____

_____

_____

_____

_____

_____

Cravings:

_____

_____

_____

_____

Pictures

Journal Page

Week 38

Appointments:

Monday	Tuesday	Wednesday	Thursday	Friday	Saturday	Sunday

Notes:

_____

_____

_____

Baby is the size of a Pumpkin

Thoughts and Feelings:

_____

_____

_____

_____

_____

_____

Cravings:

_____

_____

_____

_____

Pictures

Journal Page

Week 39

Appointments:

Monday	Tuesday	Wednesday	Thursday	Friday	Saturday	Sunday

Notes:

_____

_____

_____

Baby is the size of a Watermelon

Thoughts and Feelings:

_____

_____

_____

_____

_____

_____

Cravings:

_____

_____

_____

_____

Pictures

Journal Page

Week 40

Appointments:

Monday	Tuesday	Wednesday	Thursday	Friday	Saturday	Sunday

Notes:

_____

_____

_____

Baby is the size of a Jack Fruit

Thoughts and Feelings:

_____

_____

_____

_____

_____

_____

Cravings:

_____

_____

_____

_____

Pictures

Journal Page

It's Baby Time!

Paste 3x5 photo of baby here!

Baby's Name: _____

Date of Birth: _____ Time: _____

Weight: _____ pounds _____ ounces

Length: _____ inches

Journal Page

Journal Page

Journal Page

Journal Page

Made in the USA
Las Vegas, NV
22 November 2021

35045458R00117